A
Garden in Kentucky

A
Garden in Kentucky

poems by Jane Gentry

Louisiana State University Press
Baton Rouge and London

1995

Manufactured in the United States of America
First printing
04 03 02 01 00 99 98 97 96 95   5 4 3 2 1

Designer: Glynnis Phoebe
Typeface: Bembo
Typesetter: Impressions, a Division of Edwards Brothers, Inc.
Printer and binder: Thomson-Shore, Inc.

LIBRARY OF CONGRESS CATALOGING-IN-PUBLICATION DATA

Gentry, Jane.
   A garden in Kentucky : poems / by Jane Gentry.
      p. cm.
   ISBN 0-8071-2002-2 (cl : alk. paper). — ISBN 0-8071-2003-0 (p :
alk. paper)
   I. Title.
   PS3557.E462G37 1995
   811'.54—dc20   95-16221
                                                      CIP

The author offers grateful acknowledgment to the editors of the following publications, in which poems in this book originally appeared, sometimes in slightly different form: *Adena*, "Aunt Lucy," "Great-Grandfather's Dog, High, on a Tintype"; *America*, "Teddy"; *American Voice*, "My Mother's Clothes"; *Appalachian Heritage*, "The Cricket in the Elevator Shaft"; *Folio*, "For H., Resolved into a Moth While Watching Television in the Next Room," "A Moment in the Dark"; *Greenhouse*, "Susannah"; *Greensboro Review*, "Liberty Above New Haven: The Statue on East Rock"; *Harvard Magazine*, "By Dark," "The Drum Majorette Marries at Calvary Baptist"; *Hollins Critic*, "Epiphany, 1992," "A Garden in Kentucky," "In the Darkness," "Presences," "Washing Sheets in July"; *Humanities in the South*, "LIFE, June, 1944, Featuring the Bayeux Tapestry"; *Jar*, "Maugie's Heaven"; *Journal of Kentucky Studies*, "For My Father"; *New Virginia Review*, "Grandfather Lights the Gas Stove"; *Pikeville Review*, "Two Flowers for My Father"; *Southern Poetry Review*, "A Photograph of Hollins Abroaders Before the Caryatids"; *Spoon River Quarterly*, "Ten Years Ago You Left and Now We Take a Walk Together," "Your Vacation"; *Stonemarrow*, "Moving." "Aunt Lucy" also appeared in *Cries of the Spirit*, ed. Marilyn Sewell (Beacon Press, 1990), and in *God's Plenty: Modern Kentucky Writers*, ed. Lillie D. Chaffin, Glenn O. Carey, and Harry N. Brown (Pennkevill Publishing Co., 1991). "The Drum Majorette Marries at Calvary Baptist" also appeared in *The Night Lifted Us* (Larkspur Press, 1991). "Great-Grandfather's Dog, High, on a Tintype" also appeared in *Phrases Afternoon* (Larkspur Press, 1985), where "The Locust" appeared as well. "A Moment in the Dark" also appeared in *Ocarina: Anthology of American and World Poetry* (Boroline House, 1979). "Presences" also appeared in *Southern Writing in the Sixties*, ed. John William Corrington and Miller Williams (Louisiana State University Press, 1967). "Hound" appeared in *Intro #3*, ed. R. V. Cassill (McCall Publishing Co.; Bantam Books, 1970); and "The Whale," in *Elvis in Oz: New Stories and Poems from the Hollins Creative Writing Program* (University Press of Virginia, 1992).

The author wishes to thank the Corporation of Yaddo, the Kentucky Arts Council, the Kentucky Foundation for Women, the University of Kentucky, the Virginia Center for the Creative Arts, and the Art Group for their various gifts of attention, time, and money that supported her work on these poems.

The paper in this book meets the guidelines for permanence and durability of the Committee on Production Guidelines for Book Longevity of the Council on Library Resources. ⊗

For Louis D. Rubin, Jr.

and for my parents,
Dixie Walker Gentry
and Charles Blanding Gentry,
in the richness of memory

Mrs. Copperfield put her hand
over her heart. "Le bonheur," she
whispered, "le bonheur . . . what an
angel a happy moment is—"

—Jane Bowles, *Two Serious Ladies*

Contents

III

I

What are they looking at? Is it the river?
The sunlight on the river, the summer, leisure,
Or the luxury and nothingness of consciousness?

—Delmore Schwartz, "Seurat's 'Sunday
Afternoon Along the Seine' "

A Garden in Kentucky

Under the fluorescent sun
inside the Kroger, it is always
southern California. Hard avocados
rot as they ripen from the center out.
Tomatoes granulate inside their hides.
But by the parking lot, a six-tree orchard
frames a cottage where winter has set in.

Pork fat seasons these rooms.
The wood range spits and hisses,
limbers the oilcloth on the table
where an old man and an old woman
draw the quarter-moons of their nails,
shadowed still with dirt,
across the legends of seed catalogues.

Each morning he milks the only goat
inside the limits of Versailles. She feeds
a rooster that wakes up all the neighbors.
Through dark afternoons and into night
they study the roses' velvet mouths
and the apples' bright skins
that crack at the first bite.

When thaw comes, the man turns up
the sod and, on its underside, ciphers
roots and worms. The sun like an angel
beats its wings above their grubbing.
Evenings on the viny porch they rock,
discussing clouds, the chance of rain.
Husks in the dark dirt fatten and burst.

The Drum Majorette Marries
at Calvary Baptist

She goes blind down the aisle.
Candles prick the twilight
banks of gladioli, fern, and baby's breath.
Abloom in polyester peau de soie,
she smiles a starlet smile, clings
to her wet-eyed daddy's beef.
The organ metes her steps in groans.
Her mother wrings a tissue in her lap.
The groom, monolith to the white cloud
she is, waits at the altar. His Adam's
apple bobs. He is a straight, black
prop incidental to this script.

Outside, night falls over the tableau
the flashbulbs freeze as the couple
ducks through showers of seed
and runs for the idling limousine.
Before the door clicks shut on all her gauze,
in the strange light the white dress
seems to drift like petals piece by piece,
until out of the net the drum majorette
pumps her knees. Her trim boots dart,
her white gloves slice
at cacophonies of dark.
Her silver whistle flashes, shrills.

Grandfather Lights the Gas Stove

Grandfather breathed fire from the pulpit
and flames sat on their heads in cloven tongues.
At home, he brought white-eyed potatoes
from the pantry dark with its secret smells
of old walnuts and Bible leather.
Wearing Maugie's apron, he washed pans
and spoke earnestly to his own face
in the looking glass over the sink.

Into the bright hell of the barrel-bellied
stove, he fed the chunks of coal.
The air, sweet with heat, awash
with the clock's regular voice,
settled over us in a blessing.
Stretched on the daybed, he meditated
on the Acts of the Apostles,
the intoxicant of Pentecost. The Bible,
open across his stomach, soon rose
with his breath, his building snores.

Hooded, he comes at dawn, hunkers,
opens the valve, and the breath
of gas hisses, explodes across
the white row of teeth. Slowly
the hundreds of asbestos tongues
stir to life in the new blue fire,
and his shadow rears and leaps
across the ceiling, arches over
the cold-faced girls budding
together inside the comforter.

Maugie's Heaven

In June at sunrise robins roof
my house with nesty noises: chirrup
chirrup, the bright trees
branch into my sleep.
Once, a child on Maugie's porch,
I slept while flocks, hosts
of robins, chorused mother music
that spilled my eyes onto the bed,
the floor, the new-plowed fields
like water swelling
the year to summer.

This June new robins shout,
celebrating sky, not heaven
or lost sheep, creatures
of grass, the closed kingdom,
their bodies ripening toward
the fold that Maugie knows.
Lying deep in spring
lapped in hymns of dirt
beneath the teeth of grass,
she dreams that robins sing
their lust above her empty
house, the bed she made,
among hallelujahs of new leaves.

Aunt Lucy

As pure at ninety-four as any babe
newborn, Aunt Lucy died. She loved
a maiden's pleasures: purple, funerals,
young company, blooming hats, Jesus.
At Easter church, without an orchid
to her name, she would survey
the flowering bosoms and chastely
dream a dark-dyed purple of her own.

In Lucy's bright-eyed, backward mind,
eighty years ago was near as now: jigging
through lamplight into daylight, she frisked
her mare all day, outrode her posting,
untied beaux, until she galloped her cane to bed,
vowing she wouldn't last through winter.

Now that stones are cold, trees naked,
gardens brittle, she sleeps like a baby,
clutching a queer blossom, trundled away
under the beds of tulips and the plots of daffodils,
tucked in beneath the blank of snow
where bulbs smolder between sheets of ice.

Planted with her first and only orchid,
Lucy winters through, her old-maid mind,
feeble as February sun, recollecting snow.
Let her hold out for some combustion of that bloom
whose shoots may yet fire spring
when the cold comforter melts—
her and her rootless flower.
For they lie here and, under cover of death,
sleep a short sleep.

Great-Grandfather's Dog,
High, on a Tintype

On a sunny porch he lies,
head on paws, eyes strangely lighted,
forlorn among failing images:
empty rocker, child in the door,
sun squares on old planks.
A dog in a brown study,
he lies still in the tintype
losing itself to light.
On the back, words stay
as Maugie wrote them:
  "Papa's dog. High.
  He laid here until he died waiting for Papa.
  He would not eat. He loved him."

I see the dog
circle slowly after his tail
on the warm boards and settle
for this posture of loyalty,
bleaching now white as bones
buried in the yard.
High hoards all his bones,
bones lost to earth
bones of his master
his master's child
after the lightened breath
mumbles them all clean
after the sun's tongue
licked this picture.

The Old Place
1949

Sun pools
under the high trees
in the leafy rooms
birds crisscross
their songs.
Up the cliff, crows
fire war cries
at each other.
Men and women slap
cards on the table,
laugh, holler.
The creek
cold, mud-sucking
fresh and mossy
arcs with crawdads,
minnows. Boys
and girls skate
its slick floor
balancing like
tightrope walkers,
arms outstretched.
Pepsi-Colas frosted
in the ice chest.
Warm sweet beans,
Mary's potato salad.
Chicken fried
to crumbled bites.
Across the valley
the red-and-white barn
breathes cool
silky tobacco dust.
Around the white-
washed outhouse
mud daubers write
in terrifying loops
the script of this day
so bright, invisible.

Washing Sheets in July

Thin clouds work the sheet of sky—
jays cry, flat and starchy.
Against the white garage
hollyhocks flicker.
The sheets, wet, adhesive
as I hang them, smell
of soap and bee-filled air.

Flags of order in the palpable sun,
how they snap in the new breeze!
Watching them balloon on the line,
I swell with an old satisfaction:
I beat them clean in the Euphrates.
Poems half-conceived drift off—
unwritten essays muddle, fade.
The white sheets crack in the wind,
fat bellies of sails,
sweet as round stomachs of children.

Tonight they'll carry me to sleep
in joy, in peace,
muscles unknotting, tired eyes clearing
in the dark under their lids.
The sheets, fragrant as summer,
carry me into realms of cleanliness,
deep dreams of order.

Teddy

September sun checkers his yard.
His bearded, crowned chickens
peck and sing in the fencerow.
His angles of bone collapse
into the green yard chair;
its metal back splays like a tulip.
This moment of comfort blooms
on his slack yellow skin.

"Uncle Teddy," I say, "Daddy
has to have the operation. It is
cancer." His breath curls,
the day darkens
through the membrane of tears.
I clasp the back of his hand
on the rusty chair arm;
his five hard hand bones
separate in my palm.

For My Father

Athens, Kentucky

Bridge
When you rode in from your fields
I climbed your back
that spanned the forests of clover.
An airplane droned over us, so new
to the sky that we stopped falling and rolling
to look, shading our eyes.
There was no time then,
only that noon of blossoms, bees.

River
On the ride to the hospital
you were ruddy, joking,
pungent as your hatband.

Your roommate's leg,
numbed for a vasectomy,
fell off the bed.
You rolled out laughing
to pick it up.

A nurse ordered you down.
Wired to a gauge, your heart
became viscera.

After they brought you back
split like a melon,
I slipped into the doorframe
and saw Mother, eyes shut, in a chair
beside your head, holding
to the post of your bed,
a boat on a river
frothing, tumbling,
carrying you off.

Back
On the back porch
your coveralls slump

from their nail.
By the shed
your pickup
settles into the grass.
I rub your back.
Off the rack of your ribs
my fingers lift your skin,
an old shirt.

Hand
After the long failure of his farmer's body,
after the undertakers wrestled him,
zipped in plastic like last season's clothes,
past the kitchen table, out the back door,
and fed him into the black mouth of the hearse,
after the last warmth of his head
went out like an ember on his pillow, I left.

As a train carried me into London
I saw him look up from some hammering beside the track,
his shapeless cap pushed back.
He waved an old-gloved hand at me
familiar as sunlight
and opened his joyful smile
in a greeting I was already past.

Breath
I move away in time from where he left me.
When I am tired now, my face hangs from my checkbones;
my eyes when I catch them are sad.
This old woman hid in my bones until he died,
whose arm lifted me up
to smell the sweet breath of his horse.

After Rain
He wore weather like an old sweater,
next to his skin. He watched the sky
as one searches the face of a friend.
He heard voices in the rain on the roof.
The wind spoke to him in his own breath.

He heard the language corn speaks
growing under the July sun.
He knew the appetites of dirt,
how it eats the burst seeds.

Tonight wind thrashes the bones of trees,
and rain from the west veins my window.
All his breaths are in this wind.
The earth of his grave drinks the rain
that beats on his heart and makes it grow.
Tomorrow, within fencerows he knew
by heart (the double wild cherry,
the elm stump, the rock fence corner),
his cattle, sleek in their tight skins,
will make the grass shriek with their green teeth.

Thinking of Charlie B.
on July 4

In the city of the dead
Charlie B. is yet
a model citizen,
he who loved his life,
who loved, like a cat,
a patch of sunlight
to lie in, who wished
to be no one but himself,
to be nowhere
but where he was,
doing what he was doing.

Surely such a man
on the Fourth of July
enjoys his state,
his grave open
to all earth's weathers,
his atoms dancing
out into the summer night
to the rhythm of cicadas
singing, "Body, Body, Body,"
so black to the touch, ecstatic,
always weaving a new skin
for that old drum of darkness,
"Body, Body, Body," which marches
us all into that new city.

Snow in the Cemetery

At nightfall snow showers upon me from a sky
luminous as porcelain yellow pink.
Discrete as minutes of a heavy hour,
flakes, adhesive to my coat and scarf,
weight down dark symmetries of evergreen
and feather all the reaches of the bare-branched trees.

This accumulation freezes all I know.
And yet my mother lies in her new grave
under this blanket white and sudden
as the sheets she cracked out and smoothed
and tucked over the beds of my childhood,
peaceful as these hummocks under quiet snow.

My Mother's Clothes

On a December night
I brought them
from her nursing home,
forgot them on the porch
under stars brittle with cold.
I left them hanging, far
from the warmth
of her body, away from fires
that keep the winter from us.
Her clothes, familiar to me
as her skin: the wool plaid
dress she made; her favorite
jacket, hunter green,
with its lapel pin, DWG,
my father gave her—
the shape of the body
holding as they swung
from their shoulders
on the porch, arms empty
against the weather.

Tasks

I look in the mirror and see my father's face.
A thousand times before I've looked and seen
my own. But my father does live in the wilderness
of my heart, in a hidden cottage,
where the door sometimes opens into the vines
and he steps out to assess the sky,
to look for rain. Rarely, my mother appears
on the threshold, holding a plate or an apple.
They live there forever, moving through the day's tasks,
sacred and eternal to the eyes of a child:

> lighting the lamp
> pouring the water
> stirring the pot
> opening the window
> folding the cloth
> smoothing the bed
> drawing off the shoe

Presences

I thought my father callous, my mother hard,
and my grandfather unfeeling above all
for not being wretched when an old road moved
or when a house or barn would burn or fall.

That far child loved old things,
worshiped past because she had none.
But to change from child, she learned
as those who got her learned:
when sight goes empty through the vacant air—
the landmark gone—
its absence is more ancient than its being there.

II

I have a small
daughter called
Cleis, who is

like a golden
flower

    I wouldn't
take all Croesus'
kingdom with love
thrown in, for her

            —Sappho

A Photograph of Hollins Abroaders
Before the Caryatids

Thirty years and it will be a different picture.
Husbands do set houses on girls' heads,
hair turns as gray as rock,
and eyes in made-up faces take the stony look.
They travel but they never learn
as do those ponderous maids beneath the rock.
Worn down by the gravity of time,
but serving still, held by the common chore,
they understand the stone that keeps them down.

LIFE, June, 1944,
Featuring the Bayeux Tapestry

In a quiet courtyard, dead Germans
and the rump of a grazing horse
seen through the gap in the side of a shed.
Along a Norman beach, open graves
with two empty boots by each.
And the waves stopped by the camera.
An ad for silverware: a cottage, rose-covered,
behind a girl and her soldier holding hands,
leaning on a picket fence. They swear
they'll meet again before the sterling tarnishes.
Past all this, the feature in the back,
the record of a war sewn by a queen,
what Matilda knew of William's conquest.
Along two hundred feet of rotting linen
throngs of horses thread among each other;
amid the cotton clash of swords on shields
the warriors dump their heads along the margins,
go on needling, fighting their embroidered war.

The Cricket in
the Elevator Shaft

... sustains only a small poem:
the chirping rises
ancient as bedrock
from the pit
we dangle over
where our lifeline
crawls into its upward pull

Down there, the cricket
saws its legs,
sings
steady as stars

A Moment in the Dark

I switched off the light and put the child in bed.
As I tucked blankets round his feet, he said
in fright, finding my face with his hand,
"For a moment in the dark, Jane Gentry,
I thought you were an old lady." And
for a moment in the dark, I shall be.

For H., Resolved into a Moth While Watching Television in the Next Room

One night I was running through the backyard
of my dream, pulling from the hungry suck
of mud and tangling grass. The wind pushed hard
against strong, flapping sheets of rain that struck
and hissed upon one window filled with light.
Firm in the house's buckling, wheezing walls
which breathed the wind, a tall door took my sight,
and entering I wound straight through hollow halls.

The room, except for one bare bulb, was blank.
To nowhere, in a corner, stairs climbed high,
and at the top a tight sac flopped and sank
until a moth burst out: that monstrous fly,
as if the shaggy brown cocoon had bled,
rose damp and ruddy to batter at my head.

Hound

I am a girl of sense
and all day, as sure as sunshine,
I know you love me.
All day I stay ahead of the hound
dragging his jowls raw
to keep his nostrils in my scent.
When he snuffles up behind
I turn quick and outfox him;
my strategy's to keep him
dizzy on the daily round.
But that old dog's not dumb.
He knows the whiff of jealousy,
stays with that stench
until he tracks me down.
When I've run against the night,
am flat against my bed,
I'm forced to serve him.
Settling happy-tailed at my bedside
he ravels at my glistening guts
until we're mumbled fleshless into sleep
where love and hate are splintery bones
among the broken towers of his teeth.

Liberty Above New Haven
The Statue on East Rock

Pointing the stone needle
stitching up the looseness
of the day, she strikes against
the abstract of a sky so definitely
empty, cold, and clean
that I could wish for such a hard
and spotless place to lean.

Ten Years Ago You Left and Now We Take a Walk Together

We step
from patch to patch
of moon,
dry rocks over a spring creek.
All the mouths of night
music together.
We hold hands
familiar as crotches
of old trees.
We look through
lighted windows laughing
at the lives.
Near the end of the block
a naked woman
plump in front
of her open door
irons a shirt:
her breasts swing
over the moving heat.
We swallow the moon
what a pill
and head home.

Scarecrow

I ran you out of my garden long ago,
thought I was rid of you for good.
But now you straggle back
like a November fly bumping the cold pane.
What I married, I love:
my house, my garden, trees, children.
Yet you, ragged bird, dirty old crow,
come back here out of season,
your horny beak
slicing at my roots.
My daughter rides my leg
and hides inside my skirt.
My husband is cast down,
picks at his supper, skulks.
The dog and cats
tuck tails between their legs
and sniff their food.
Only you, gobbler,
ransack, ravage, waste our garden.
You stick like a fly at the eye
of a cow in August
until I hang a pie tin in the tree,
an empty eye to knife sun into you,
and dress a man of sticks
in my ruffled purple blouse
you always liked,
my husband's hat and work gloves dangling.
The scarecrow stands there
and, death for his familiar,
cannot die. He serves.
You come no more.

Blizzard

Tonight snow
showers flake
by flake through
the streetlight's
funnel, settles
its particulars
in billows
that snake around
the island
of our house
in the white dark.

Quiet in bed
under rafters
that float the weight
of snow above us
we drift
from this warm orbit
wave after wave
we cross into each
other, seep
into the void
particles colliding
dancing Shiva's dance
dreaming the dream
of the eye seeing
all itself
blinded in sleep
wind hurls the light
flakes into white surfs
stretching the empty fields
around our house.

Morning comes and a wash of blue
fire carries us home
from every facet of the world
crystal splinters arrow the eye
the day's one sun we always rise to.

Moving

Going back
to sweep up
broken crayons, brown
apple cores, nail parings,
I feel the ghosts
fritter in the clear
space where the sofa was,
dissolve into the wall
where the refrigerator stood.
The whites of my eyes see
them shift about the ceiling.

With all we own
gone, puzzled
like a jigsaw in the van,
the empty rooms hold
what we can't clear out
and leave here.

Your Vacation

Your absence floods the house
like dark at night
washing through closets, drawers, boxes,
seeping between the clock and the wall,
books and their spines

and my need sings
out on it
like these cicadas
screaming
behind banks of summer's black old leaves.

Susannah

I
Beetle on its back,
hooked fish on the bank,
paddling through air
in her crib,
she reaches out.
Seeing my breasts,
her eyes light
at known geography.

I am
what
I am:
perfect answer
to her appetite.
Empty O
of her mouth
eats my nipple,
her quick tongue flickers,
a snake in its hole.

The suck
of her
deep kiss
pulls me in,
she draws me,
tide to moon.
I flow to her,
locks open
I fall
to her level
in peace.

II
I rode the pig
push
when she came,

grunt, grunt
root, root
an animal snorted
deep in the swell
of my gut,
wave after wave
till sluices
opened
and out through my circles
she poured.

A sac she'd filled,
I ricocheted
around that room,
an emptying balloon
on the loose
caroming
off the cold lights,
battering at the green–
masked faces,
riding the red jet
her body washed
from mine.

III
Susannah
is
the name
I give this vacancy
this vacuum
I rush into
like wind
scrolled into thunder
when lightning scribbles
voids
across the sky.
Bug, fish, snake, pig,
she is
primordial.
In the jelly of her flesh
there is no bone.

I am
her spine, her shell,
her wing, her teeth,
her beak, her claw.

In love she breaks me
over the back
of the dark
she came from.

Susannah's Bones

When she was newborn
the hard S of her body
cracked, the vertebrae
giving as I lifted her.

I thought I'd dropped a stitch,
had let my faults undo her—
the getting too offhand,
milk scanted, vitamins missed.

For years, then, my sleep
listened for her bones.
At 3 A.M. she'd find me
in the dark, whispering,

"Mama," filling the black room.
But as her small body tossed
beside me, while I fought dreams
of fault in the marrow,

her bone knobs bloomed,
her white joints flowered
like popped corn. Her sockets
succulent, tender kernels.

St. Lucy the Housekeeper

Today I wash my windows inside
to make the most of the year's old sun.
With my own hands I keep this house,
live quietly, darkly, day by day,
sometimes finding casements open
onto odd landscapes, pasts not mine,
the empty walls cracking
in zigzags like eggs.

December is my season,
winter's dark when I was born.
Then my house draws close its shawl
of dust, images flower the walls,
my viny rugs grow lush,
and my rich old relative, Memory,
dies, pouring into my apron
bright new-minted coin.

Zero

The temperature is five above.
From the attic window
I see rooftops dimming
in the last light. The wind sulks,
cut by old bones of trees
which yearn like grass
into the moving sky.
Snow rains.
Streetlights awaken here, now there.
A front window lamp winks on.
Night falls like black water.
Against the world's shapes
and the warm human interiors
darkness at this moment shows its face.

Things That Fly Overhead
at Lake Malone

In the dark, on my back
on the sun-warmed dock,
I am surprised by what comes
between me and the night sky's
obsolete face.
A plane's red eye winks.
Its rumble burrs a comfort
to the sharp songs of the tree frogs.
A bat boomerangs after gnats, sometimes
so close I make out horns and pointed wings.
Then, way up, a firefly fades, so deep in black
I see it first as a star, light-years away.

Leaving Lucy, September, 1990

"You'll never have to worry
about that one," Jean once said,
as Lucy, the princess
in my prom dress
and bridesmaid's tiara,
squared herself between
the timid ghost and cat
to receive her treat
at the dark door.

This afternoon I leave her
in New York. I am ready.
Her new comforter is on her bed.
Her texts are bought and stand
like a rainbow on her shelf.

At the hotel, we close our bags,
find the key, double-check her schedule.
She cries beside her father on the sofa.
Because my body hollows and my hands
begin to flame, I leave the room.
I say I'll look under the beds.

Alone, I sink into the bed.
The room blackens around me.
My eyes fall
into their own emptiness.
I am a child. Long ago
someone is leaving me alone.
It is dark. A door closes.
Cicadas shake the night trees.

Lucy meets me in the doorway,
come to see what's wrong.
The tears we cry are old.
We are not two bodies.

As I pull away from the curb
she blurs. Her shape
in the rearview mirror
moves toward its own door.

In a Chinese Landscape

From the creek the bullfrog's voice opens the night
cicadas scrape the rhythm of dog days
out of the dry trees the moon climbs
into the purple of evening.
Far away my father lies withering on his bed.

My heart is full as the moon's circle
now orange and palpable
it will rise and the dark will swallow it
shrinking to a sliver
in the shadow of earth.

Two Flowers for My Father

That spring there were floods.
The summer was dry as a fever.
In October, fall still hadn't come
when the undertaker hauled his body
out under the close stars.

Now tobacco sweetens the air
of the creek bottom. Ice curdles
the barnlot puddles.
But on the back hill, a Queen Anne's lace
frames its bloody center in a clutch of briers,
and between hedge roots on the creek bank
a snapdragon, blue and deep
as sky, opens its old throats.

On a Day of Beautiful Clouds

. . . after three days of rain, I drive east
on I-64 into a sky broken open like an egg,
pouring a shine new as the first day
into my eyes. The trees, fat with summer
rain, bulge over the road, then open
to a tent of sky as blue as sea, where
just above the landline, separate clouds
swim like fish into ultramarine.
Straight up, the scrubbed-out sky
is clean as the yellow-washed world
that rolls beneath my tires.
I pass a man, white-headed, grand as God,
standing in a yard as rapt, relieved,
absorbed as if in pissing, his face lighted,
wiped clear by this depth of sky, this beaming.

III

. . . what every child knows: that nothing is ever
suffered in plural.
There is only one body. Only one death.

—Stephen Mitchell, "Pascal's Vision"

Telemakhos at Festival Market
Thinks of His Father

How strange that your bones, four blocks away
under these rosy, peaceful clouds,
carried upon themselves the familiar
house of my childhood, your body.
Your oar may as well have been a winnowing fan
for all the good it finally did you.
Only the lost know your words as truth:
though you find a house of gold,
it cannot be as sweet as your own house
or the house of your parents.
Now as I eat my supper in this mall
I listen to the murmur of artificial
falls and to the tunes Calliope plays
as she turns some children on the carrousel.
I, too, find myself upon a promontory,
not as you were on Ogygia, alone,
trying to break the blue distance with the naked
eye, but, high above the street, I look down
into the laps of strangers by the carful
rolling past one another at Main and Broadway,
where you, when you were young, ate lunch, shot pool.
Across Triangle Park, in the glass grid
of the Hyatt, travelers light the same lamp
over and over. Boys with half heads-of-hair
ride skateboards down recirculating fountains.
Here, you are already strange.
Under the sunset shifting and serene
you lie in an ancient town
sinking, lost as Troy.

Eleuthera

blue folds
waves

fall white
on the white beach
hissing
black weed
snakes

white stacks
cloud
the far sea
edge

the black man
drops his hammer

among the sharp
thick tongues
of foliage

looses his clothes
runs shining on the white
sand, kicking water

blue blossoms
lick his body
galloping
rising falling

eruptions of jet

Flood

Big Spring Park
February, 1991

In the wind of your mouth
I sucked a moon with a face
like the town clock.

In your darkness I drank
a black wine studded
with lax old berries.

On the muddy path
I find half a pencil
and think I'll write

these lines to you.
But, pulp to the lead,
it shatters. I fling

it on the water
with a curse: these
yellow shards, may

this cold swollen rock-
knocking stream hurl
them straight into
the bull's-eye of your heart.

Eros

Who are you?
In deepest night you come
into my bedroom wearing
your delicious boy's body.
I think of graying Sappho
crisscrossing the Aegean
searching for you
as you fled before her.
Bite by bite, my mouth
and body taste your pungency
sweet on the tongue
as salt and satisfaction.
On my black bed
our hungers eat away
our flesh, yours young,
mine not quite
old, until our bones
slide against each other
naked and unhinged,
as alike in this dark room
as seeds inside maracas.
This rattling of our bones:
a percussion, a music!
I sink into my sleep
again without a candle.

In the Darkness

The body asks its own questions.
My skin yearns toward yours.
My mind has folded itself like wings
into the egg and disappeared.

My flesh gorges, slacks, and translates
into flame, though it makes no sense
and is not real. I am tough-minded.

But at your touch my brain blooms
black red like the night inside
your mouth: a rose that never
goes to seed opens its petals furred
like pelts pulsing with dark blood.
Your tongue swells with what it cannot
utter, ancient utterings my tongue takes.

By the Sea: The Dream
of the Body

To know what it wants.
Always to have what it wants,
like a spoiled baby, plump, luxuriant,
always the center of a circle of admirers.
No past, no future, just the zero
of this moment. One perfect day
on the island of Eleuthera
I, in my fifty-first year,
ride a bike along a bright
sun-dappled lane as if I were
a ten-year-old who thinks
somebody fifty nearly dead.
The air lifts my sweaty hair
and fills the cells that build
my skin. Gravity, inertia
curl in my wake.
Suddenly, through the vegetation,
I can see into the depths of sky
and blue, blue ocean. Flying
down this road tented
by the wind-bent casserinas,
I cannot see the end
of them. They stretch
beyond my death, beyond
the swelling, falling of the sea,
like breath; beyond the movement
of pine needles among each other,
like voices; beyond the tremblings
of live sky above them, like young
sex, when the body knows
each pore's single appetite.
The body is the island,
the garden. Our hunger is itself
the fruit (apples, mangoes, all
that is sweet and succulent)

that dangles into reach.
Oh stretch the suppleness
of every joining in your body
toward that fruit. Eat.
Make death, and undo it.

Epiphany, 1992

I went out into the frigid night
to shift cars in the driveway.
Finished I looked up into the clear
black distances of Orion hunting
in circles through the dark,
his leg thrown over the horizon.

If only I could empty myself
of you and your absence.

No. Then you would be lost
as if you'd never been
climbing the dark with the stars,
striding with your black dog
across the winter sky brilliant
because it is void and cold.

Janus

The mud of January,
cold ooze shining
out in the open rain
for ten straight dark days.

Under it the bodies of people
I have loved lie papery, unreal,
and bulbs that will be narcissus,
tulips, daffodils, hold their own
against rot and freezing.

Dirt. If I open the door
of my skin, there
it is, pulsing, glistening,
only itself, implacable.

The Whale

Purple, languid, content, cruising
the ocean bottom, land without light;
behemoth fueled by a cumulus shifting breath
rolled in its lungs delicious as smoke
in the addict's mouth, but having at last
to break the membrane of the surface to take
air. So while I peel potatoes, or bend
to switch the channel on the car radio, grief
may without warning break my face,
my everyday skin. Because there was
a summer day when the clouds overhead
like magic slates rewrote themselves in silence,
because the falling chatter of the chimney swifts
at twilight sank tighter and tighter into circles
of darkness, I know that the world does speak,
but in all its tongues each word means good-bye.

On a Perfect Day

. . . I eat an artichoke in front
of the Charles Street Laundromat
and watch the clouds bloom
into white flowers out of
the building across the way.
The bright air moves on my face
like the touch of someone who loves me.
Far overhead a dart-shaped plane softens
through membranes of vacancy. A ship,
riding the bright glissade of the Hudson, slips
past the end of the street. Colette's vagabond
says the sun belongs to the lizard
that warms in its light. I own these moments
when my skin like a drumhead stretches on the frame
of my bones, then swells, a bellows filled
with sacred breath seared by this flame,
                                    this happiness.

A Glimpse

Just a glimpse down the side street
as I speed past on Maxwell.
In my vision no more than two
seconds: he and she
in a front yard. His arms,
wrapped as if around a trunk
he climbs, pull her up
to his mouth, his legs planted
in the grass on either
side of hers, unlike in
advertisements where
postures make a dance
of appetite. No.
Here he bends onto
her, and she, face open
and straight up, meets
him full on as if each
one has crossed a desert,
or lasted out a long, long drought.
One is rod, one is rock.
In their mouths, from
their tongues, spring waters.

In the Kroger: For Jim,
His Daughter Dead in a Wreck

Last night your beautiful child rose
into my sight as I looked from my window
at the blooming apple tree in moonlight.

Today at the store I came upon you
by the cereal shelf struck
like a monument, so hard and real
your bones shone like marble
or alabaster, bright arcs of grief.

Before the wreck when I saw you
with your cart, a different man
stood in your dark suit,
your everyday skin, that hide
we all wear. Now
you light the aisle.
Your bones, old moon slivers.

The Sudden Appearance of Love
Marco Island, Florida

The canal blackens under the sunset,
glitters with shards of fire
flung into mosaic on its moving skim.
Like tapestries unfurled from tableaux
of ruby clouds, the water tempts me
to step off the dock and walk.

Suddenly, out of the dark underwater
a fish, not big, not beautiful
(a mullet or a jack), leaps,
shattering viscosity
into scales of light, smacks
the air as with an open hand
showering iridescence
on the broken floor.
Circles widen into black horizons.

By Dark

Out of the blue
a black boomerang,
a gull's shadow
drops to the beach.
I walk at water's edge
as far as I can go
and still get home by dark.
Returning, I step
in my own footprints,
a new way back.

Aubade

At daybreak a crow's hard cry
breaks apart the darkness,
which disappears black
feather by black feather.

February 23, in the Cemetery

The first blue sky since December
today arches over me.
Late sun strikes the holly leaves,
waxy and burnished.
Two rabbits turn figure eights
among the tombstones.
Two sparrows tumble on the dead grass
in their mating flurry.
A crow as still as the stone of the urn
he stands on: the black triangle of his beak,
            the black star of his eye.

Exercise in the Cemetery

At dusk I walk up and down
among the rows of the dead.
What do the thoughts I think
have to do with another living being?
In the eastern sky, blue-green as a bird's egg,
a cloud with a neck like a goose
swims achingly toward the zenith.

Heike's Window at Nightfall, from Versailles Cemetery

Perhaps the dead can see in Heike's window
and, after dark at dinnertime, sit
upon their stones in rows mesmerized
as at a picture show, watching
through the narrow glass, slivers
of lives: Irwin's arm reaching
a jug of tea; Harck's boy arm extending
a cup that water fills; Heike
capping berries at the sink, then lifting out
the bread the toaster raises. These gestures
fascinate the dead who watch that glass
as unforgiving and as hard as molten sands
they've crossed. On my own path
falls the light from Heike's window,
a flattened, grave-shaped shining
I step into.

The Locust

. . . is an ugly virgin
plain daughter
favorless and poor.
But when May comes
and birds sing wedding songs
the country shines, the locust blooms,
a white bride
vulgar with promise.

She roots in dirt.
From dirt she draws her ugliness
and spins the veil that covers
dirt that rises, branches
to this flowering of dirt
sweetening the air,
rounding the sky
with blossoms.

In the Moment of My Death:
For My Father

You were simple, I suppose,
delighted by life
so that sickness and death
came to you as a surprise
out of the shadows of your heart.

In the moment of my death
may your old happiness light my way,
and the image of your face
smiling, happy at my coming,
be a lantern in the dark.

Hungry Fire

for J.J.F., 1941–1990

Everything becomes fire, and from fire everything is born.
—Herakleitos

Home is where one starts from. As we grow older
The world becomes stranger, the pattern more complicated
Of dead and living. Not the intense moment
Isolated, with no before and after,
But a lifetime burning in every moment.
—T. S. Eliot, *Four Quartets*

The flames ate the house from the bottom up,
sought with their tongues around the chimney,
then devoured whole an order of place, time,
and generations: Sparta, Kentucky, 1990,
the infinite regression of mothers and fathers
from the single person, only child—
James Joiner Fielder, 49 years old the week before,
the age his father died. We predicted
the fire: he drank himself to sleep most nights,
after stoking to red heat his wood stove;
he baked tuna casserole from his own recipe
or fried steaks at three in the morning,
leaving the burner on, forgetting to eat;
the wiring, new in 1927, frayed, unraveled.
When his mother, Hope, died, he divided
himself in two and piece by piece gave all
her things away: the cut-glass punch bowl,
"before some bastard steals it," the pillow-
cases from her bed, embroidered by Aunt Molly:
"Go to Sleep like the Flowers"; her jewelry,
her clothes. His own things he kept,
though there was little room for him in the house.
He farmed as well as Pick, our grandfather,
better than his uncles. He knew where his ground
was rich. His big-leafed tobacco grew taller
than his neighbors' because he knew when rain
was coming and set his plants in time.

He loved machinery—the older, the more
useless, the better: the Case steam engine
Pick bought in 1919, the thresher from the thirties,
the metal-wheeled tractor from the twenties,
and the '42 Ford cattle truck, sunk to the rims
behind the barn, its cab grown full of ragweeds.
He spent his last afternoon on his John Deere,
pulling his brand-new wagon around and around
the two blocks of Sparta. The men at the store
shook their heads, laughed, admired the wagon.
He always wanted Hope to watch him. If he went
to Southern States in Winchester to buy a part
he'd call her twice, at least, before returning.
And twice during the year of her small strokes
she came downstairs in the morning to find
a Sparta boy in his bed on the side porch.
She asked her cousin once, a worldly man
in from the army, "Can you tell me exactly
what a homosexual is and if I know any?"
As they looked out over the long lawn
toward the draw-chain gate, he answered, "No,"
she knew none. But with all this,
the fire still stunned us, a catastrophe
unthinkable, yet simply an explosion
into the present moment of the workings
of the years, the entropy of this peculiar order.

But in this house the order, though old,
was fresh still, undiscovered and guarded
by his ownership: in the parlor secretary
the letters to Pick about his sons' drinking
and cockfighting, from wise Dr. Lovell
who birthed them all; in the dining-room
press the twelve tin cups of the picnic set
that went to Boone's Creek on Sundays;
Lily's iron skillets and pots on wide shelves
in the back-porch pantry, among the ranks
of canning jars; the packet of blue-backed deeds
in the desk under the front stairs tracing
the ownerships and boundaries of seven farms
Pick gave his sanity and strongest years
to getting for his children; the stack

of unquilted quilt tops Lily made from pieces
of their worn-out best ("Something from nothing,"
she always said); all the lacework, the fine-
stitched nightgowns and petticoats laid
in tissue in the cedar chest Uncle Walter built
in the penitentiary; the black pages
of photographs, some the only remnant of faces
once as familiar as our own in the mirror—
all broken, rendered into elements,
inchoate ashes, by those bright tongues
that made each room a hell to bring
the house down into its own foundations.
It settled finally into the rock hole that held it up
and defined those spaces where we walked in air,
those lifted rooms that held our lives' beginnings.

At first it hissed. It could have been put out then.
Then it crackled as it fueled past return, then
it sang and roared in the destruction
that he required of his sin, depriving us
(heirs, too, as he was) of secrets written
in the secret order of this house. He blamed
us for our impotence to save him from sodomy
there on the dining-room floor
under the watchful faces of Hope's Haviland
looking down from their places in the cupboard.
Before he passed out loathing himeself, he paid
Randy Perkins, already having forgotten the wave,
the irresistible wave of desire that rolled over
him always unexpectedly, carrying him away
from himself, away from the order Hope left
him in the hope that it could save him.

As Virgil writes, "Gods of my country!
I follow, and where you lead there I shall be!
Preserve my house, preserve my little grandson! . . .
                    And now we heard the roar
Of the fire grow louder and louder through the town
And the waves of heat rolled nearer ever nearer."
On that first springlike day, smoke and heat
still wavered into the clear March sky
from the hopscotch of rubble I prodded through:

a stack of pink-flowered saucers melted together;
the blackened shards of the meat platter; a few
orange and blue flowers of the Chinese tea set
that stood in its tray on the sideboard
the eight years since Hope died;
the blue enamel tea kettle filled with water
from the firemen's hoses, still in its spot
inside the kitchen fireplace; the nested
tablespoons fused, rusted, their silver gone;
his brand-new typewriter, the keyboard
bones of flimsy fingers warped by heat.
This is ruin, what comes of siege, invasion:
not one stone left upon another. Shining
towers, broad streets: the eastern windows
that caught the morning sun and threw it back
to travelers on the road; the cool, generous
hall where the spiral stairs lifted; the parlor
where sunlight pooled through the bay window
onto the bright garden of the old carpet.
The company-best of that room dismantled
by the quick ferocity of flames:
Pick's life-size portrait, heavy in gold leaf,
hanging beside the framed papers of Thunder,
his Walker foxhound. Twisted metal, the stem
of the organ lamp, its globed roses exploded,
marks their places. The books stood in the shelf
as the glass shattered in front of them: *The Royal
Road to Romance, Songs That Never Die,* the volumes
of *The American Educator,* the Bible where Lily
recorded in her veiny script births, marriages,
deaths, the time of day, the dates, the years.
The coffin-shaped Steinway, its legs thick
as elephants', all its strings snapped, tangled
in the cellar hole, collapsed into the pit.

Prodding with the bent poker he used last night
to stir his logs, I lifted and turned all the pieces
I could move, searching for whatever might remain,
for something left intact that might raise the house
again, reorder in their orbits the scattered atoms
that made the pattern here. I longed to find
Harmonia's necklace, the one beautiful thing

intact, a miracle of survival in the ruins
from which could be drawn all that was lost at Thebes,
fractal of the wholeness here dissolved:
the circle of talk around the bedroom fireplace
winter nights; the talk of women, white and black,
shelling peas for canning on a summer morning;
Lily singing "Amazing Grace," thinking of a grave
at Black's Station while she ironed; he, Johnnie,
and I at hide-and-seek, racing out into the cold
rooms from the safe hub of women at the hearth:
"A bushel of wheat, a bushel of rye,
all not ready, holler I!"

Finally in the white ash of the kitchen
the firemen at daylight uncovered his
body curled in its first posture
on the floor beside the oven. Nearby
I pried up the overturned sink cabinet
and found, still in the wire drainer,
his supper plate, without a chip or smudge,
of the blue-willow set Lily bought in 1917,
as noted in her diary, from a traveling salesman.
He washed his plate and fork, perhaps his last
act of order, put Silly and Marie, his dogs, outside
to safety, perhaps as Randy, needing money,
was walking in the kitchen door.

On my shelf of blue glass, the plate now stands
indistinguishable except to those who may see
in it a blaze of balance, of wholeness,
a family rooted in a place of dusty paths,
dirt roads with grass down the middle, of barns,
gardens, neighbors, cattle, itself a miraculous
duration, itself rare, not its loss. For in that plate's
round continence, three small blue men among blue
trees, flowers, houses, cross a blue bridge
toward the sea, toward distant mountains, a comfort.
Deep in its scene, far beneath its glaze,
on the other side of the world in fact, stands
a white house. Its windows catch the morning
sun among green trees where guineas will clatter
themselves to sleep in the long peaceful fire of sunset.